W9-CMF-678

I See Yellow

Trudy Micco

Bailey Books
an imprint of
Enslow Publishers, Inc.
40 Industrial Road
Box 398
Berkeley Heights, NJ 07922
USA
http://www.enslow.com

Bailey Books, an imprint of Enslow Publishers, Inc.

Library of Congress Cataloging-in-Publication Data

Micco, Trudy.
I see yellow / Trudy Micco.
p. cm. — (All about colors)
Summary: "Learn about the color yellow"— Provided by publisher.
Includes bibliographical references and index.
ISBN 978-0-7660-3790-8
1. Yellow—Juvenile literature. 2. Color—Juvenile literature. I. Title.
QC495.5.M478 2011
535.6—dc22
                              2010011881

Paperback ISBN: 978-1-59845-165-8

Printed in the United States of America

062010 Lake Book Manufacturing, Inc., Melrose Park, IL

10 9 8 7 6 5 4 3 2 1

To Our Readers: We have done our best to make sure all Internet Addresses in this book
were active and appropriate when we went to press. However, the author and the publisher
have no control over and assume no liability for the material available on those Internet sites
or on other Web sites they may link to. Any comments or suggestions can be sent by e-mail
to comments@enslow.com or to the address on the back cover.

♻ Enslow Publishers, Inc., is committed to printing our books on recycled paper. The paper
in every book contains 10% to 30% post-consumer waste (PCW). The cover board on the
outside of each book contains 100% PCW. Our goal is to do our part to help young people
and the environment too!

Photo Credits: Shutterstock.com

Cover Photo: Shutterstock.com

Note to Parents and Teachers
Help pre-readers get a jumpstart on reading. These lively stories introduce simple concepts
with repetition of words and short simple sentences. Photos and illustrations fill the pages
with color and effectively enhance the text. Free Educator Guides are available for this series
at www.enslow.com. Search for the *All About Colors* series name.

Contents

Words to Know

duck

yellow

Where is my yellow duck?

Is my yellow duck here?

No!

Is my yellow
duck here?

No!

Is my yellow
duck here?

No!

Is my yellow duck here?

No!

Is my yellow duck here?

No!

Is my yellow
duck here?

No!

Here is my yellow duck!

**My yellow duck
is here with me!**

Read More

Bruce, Lisa. *Yellow*. Chicago, Ill.: Raintree, 2004.

Gordon, Sharon. *Yellow*. New York: Benchmark Books, 2005.

Web Sites

Do2Learn. *Colors.*
<http://www.dotolearn.com/games/whatcolor/pages/index.html>

Enchanted Learning. *I Love Color: Shades of Yellow.*
<http://www.enchantedlearning.com/colors/yellow.shtml>

Index

Guided Reading Level: B
Guided Reading Leveling System is based on the guidelines
recommended by Fountas and Pinnell.

Word Count: 59